Grevy's Zebra New Zealand Bushwren White-Necked Crow Smoky Mouse Spanish Imperial Eagle Northern Aplomado Falcon
Andrew's Frigatebird Diana Monkey Coastal California Gnatcatcher False Water Rat Slender-billed Kite
Imperial Parrot Bridled White-Eye Hispid Hare Swinhoe's Pheasant Leopard
Piping Plover Pygmy Chimpanzee Guam Rail Blunt-Nosed Leopard Lizard Florida Grasshopper Sparrow Western Whipbird
Tristram's Woodpecker Jaguarundi Chinese Alligator Virgin Islands Tree Boa Palila Honeycreeper African Dwarf Crocodile Fiji Crested
Iguana Sao Miguel Bullfinch Gambel's Watercress Desert Monitor Giant Garter Snake Ponape Greater White-Eye Flattened Musk Turtle
Guam Micronesian Kingfisher Apache Trout Spotted Pond Turtle Brown Pelican Shenandoah Salamander African Viviparous
Toad Mexican Blindcat St. Vincent Parrot Saint Francis' Satyr Butterfly Duskytail Darter Pecos Gambusia Smoky Madtom Mauritius
Cuckoo-Shrike Rio Grande Silvery Minnow Delta Smelt Burmese Peacock Turtle Little Colorado Spinedace Tiger Shortnose Sucker
Saudi Arabian Gazelle Southern Acornshell Ivory-Billed Woodpecker Inflated Heelsplitter Alabama Lampmussel Morro
Bay Kangaroo Rat Carter's Mustard Mexican Long-Nosed Bat Higgins' Eye Pearlymussel Fat Pocketbook Warm Springs Pupfish Laysan
Finch Southern River Otter Stirrupshell Tahiti Flycatcher Kanab Ambersnail Flat-Spired Three-Toothed Snail Tooth Cave Ground Beetle
Chihuahua Chub Bolson Tortoise Mitchell's Satyr Butterfly Atitlan Grebe Kern Primrose Sphinx Moth Socorro Isopod Riverside Fairy Shrimp
San Mateo Thornmint Florida Panther Island Night Lizard Hook-Billed Hermit Ash Meadows Milk-Vetch
Cape Fear Shiner Truckee Barberry Utah Prairie Dog Awikiwiki Pitcher's Thistle Schaus Swallowtail Butterfly Bunched Cory
Cactus Terlingua Creek Cats-Eye Haha Leafy Prairie-Clover Dwarf Wedge Mussel Black Lace Cactus African Elephant
San Diego Button-Celery Arabian Ostrich Contra Costa Wallflower Minnesota Dwarf Trout-Lily Sand Skink Clay's Hibiscus
Snail Darter Slender Rush-Pea Brazilian Three-Toed Sloth Tasmanian Forester Kangaroo Prairie Bush-Clover Michaux's
Sumac Mississippi Sandhill Crane Banbury Springs Limpet Fine-Rayed Pigtoe Clay-Loving Wild-Buckwheat Texas Snowbells
Great Indian Rhinoceros Bumblebee Bat Ashy Dogweed Greenback Cutthroat Trout Giant Panda Helmeted Honeyeater Chinese
River Dolphin West African Manatee Sacramento Prickly-Poppy Black-Footed Cat Guadeloupe House Wren San Joaquin Kit Fox Brush-
Tailed Rat-Kangaroo Tooth Cave Spider Gibbon Stock Island Tree Snail Crested Honeycreeper Jamaican Boa Lion-Tailed Macaque
Black-Footed Ferret Campbell Island Flightless Teal Godfrey's Butterwort Gray Wolf Pyrenean Ibex Bactrian Camel
Gelada Baboon Appalachian Monkeyface Pearlymussel Ruth's Golden Aster Hooded Crane Nile Crocodile Cameroon Clawless Otter
American Black Bear Cook's Holly Aquatic Box Turtle Welsh's Milkweed Sandplain Gerardia Ka'u Silversword Vahl's Boxwood Papery
Whitlow-Wort Hawaiian Bluegrass Dwarf Naupaka Sneed Pincushion Cactus Leedy's Roseroot Shapo
Andean Condor Pink-Headed Duck Spreading Avens Western Prairie Fringed Orchid Neosho Madtom White Irisette
Cui-ui Slender-Petaled Mustard Mugger Crocodile Clouded Leopard Radiated Tortoise Tennessee Yellow-Eyed Grass
Louisiana Quillwort Giant Scops Owl Resplendent Quetzel Least Tern Barrington Land Iguana Desert Dace
Pygmy Sculpin Bliss Rapids Snail Oregon Silverspot Butterfly Tooth Cave Pseudoscorpion Razorback Sucker
Peacock Softshell Turtle Salt Marsh Harvest Mouse Little Planigale Hawaiian Stilt Nightjar Sand Gazelle Marsh Deer
Andean Cat Long-Tailed Otter Puerto Rican Boa Orangutan Hawaiian Monk Seal Uakari Hawaiian Coot

GENESIS

ART BY ED YOUNG

ADAPTED FROM THE KING JAMES VERSION

A Laura Geringer Book

An Imprint of HarperCollins*Publishers*

AUTHOR'S NOTE

To me Genesis represents the very beginning of all possibility—the energy that is the seed of life. Rather than rendering a literal interpretation of the text, I have tried to capture this spirit of fluidity, of life in its variations and transformations, in my artwork—as you turn each page, the heavens, the earth, the land, the sea, the marine and land animals, emerge from the shadows, each a part of the next, until finally, there is man.

The endpapers are composed of the names of hundreds of endangered and extinct animals, with those that are extinct highlighted; for I also see in Genesis a gentle reminder that the earth is ours to protect.

For George Levenson

Genesis
Copyright © 1997 by Ed Young.
Printed in the U.S.A. All rights reserved.

Library of Congress Cataloging-in-Publication Data
Bible. O.T. Genesis. English. Young. 1997.
  Genesis / art by Ed Young ; adapted from the King James version.
    p.   cm.
  "A Laura Geringer book."
  ISBN 0-06-025356-8. — ISBN 0-06-025357-6 (lib. bdg.)
  [1. Creation.] I. Young, Ed. II. Title.
BS1233.Y68 1997   94-18698
222'.1105209—dc20   CIP
                                AC

Typography by Tom Starace
1 2 3 4 5 6 7 8 9 10
❖
First Edition

GENESIS

In the beginning God created the heaven and the earth. And the earth was without form, and void; and darkness was upon the face of the deep.

And God said, Let there be light: and there was light.

And God saw the light, that it was good: and God divided
the light from the darkness.

And God called the light Day, and the darkness he called
Night. And the evening and the morning were the first day.

And God said, Let there be a firmament in the midst of the waters, and let it divide the waters from the waters.

And God called the firmament Heaven. And the evening and the morning were the second day.

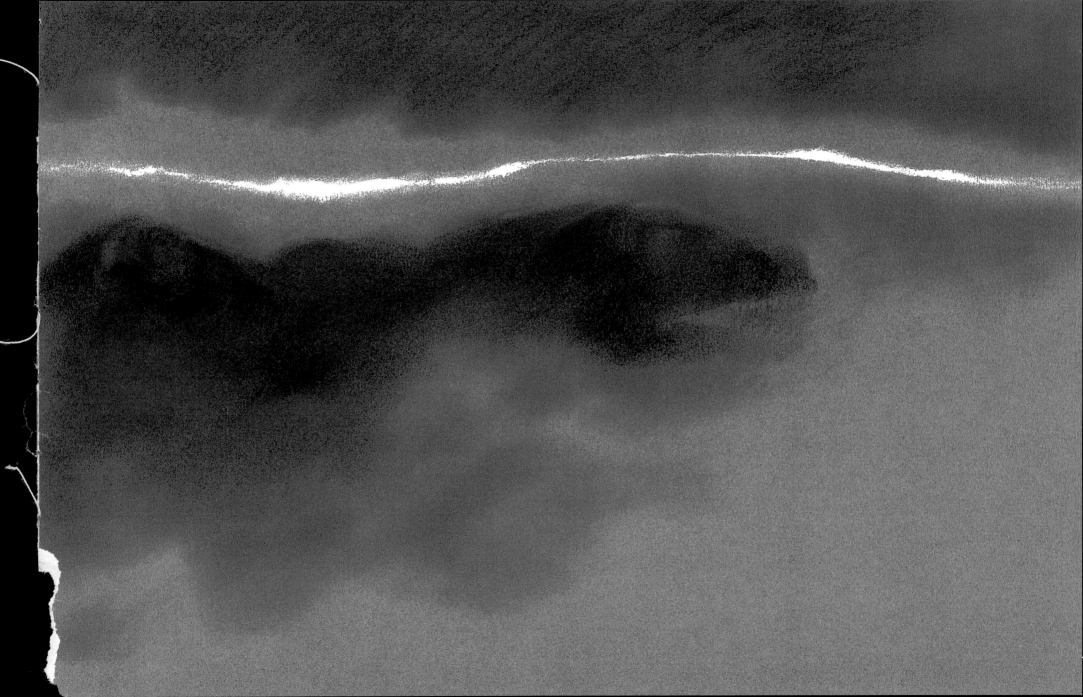

And God said, Let the waters under the heaven be gathered together unto one place, and let the dry land appear.

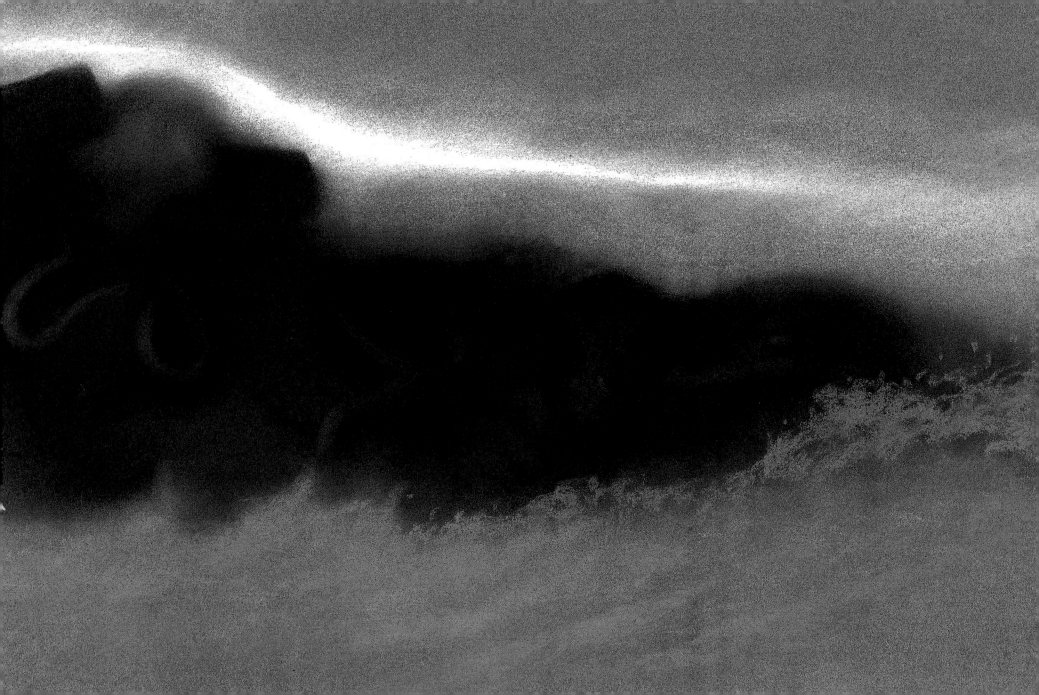

And God called the dry land Earth; and the gathering together of the waters called he Seas: and God saw that it was good.

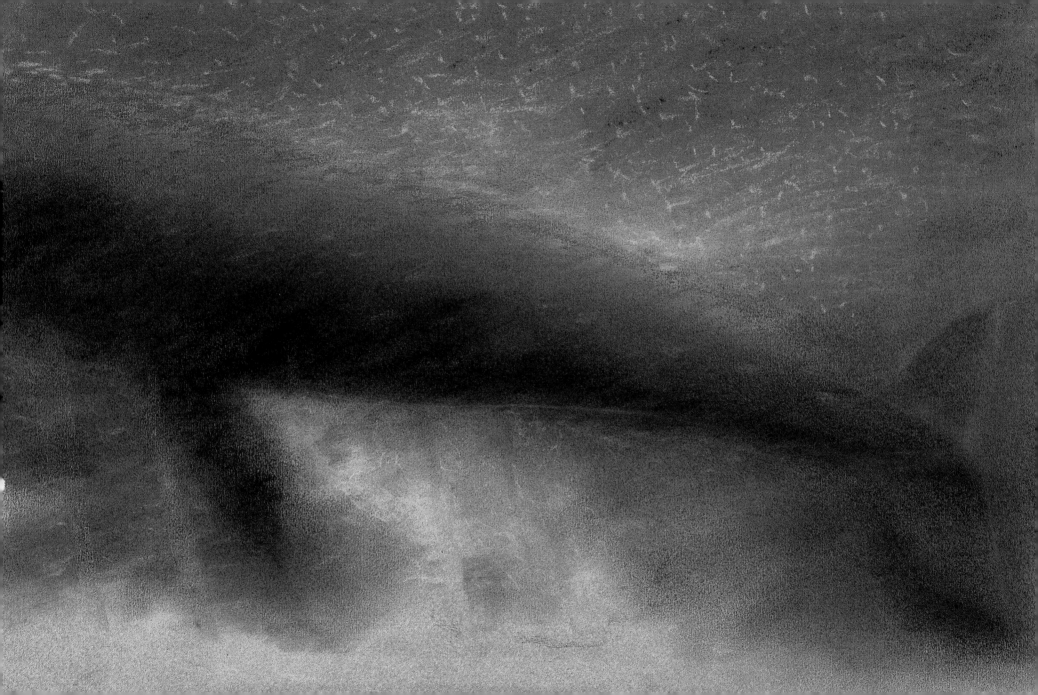

And God said, Let the earth bring forth grass, the herb yielding seed, and the fruit tree yielding fruit:

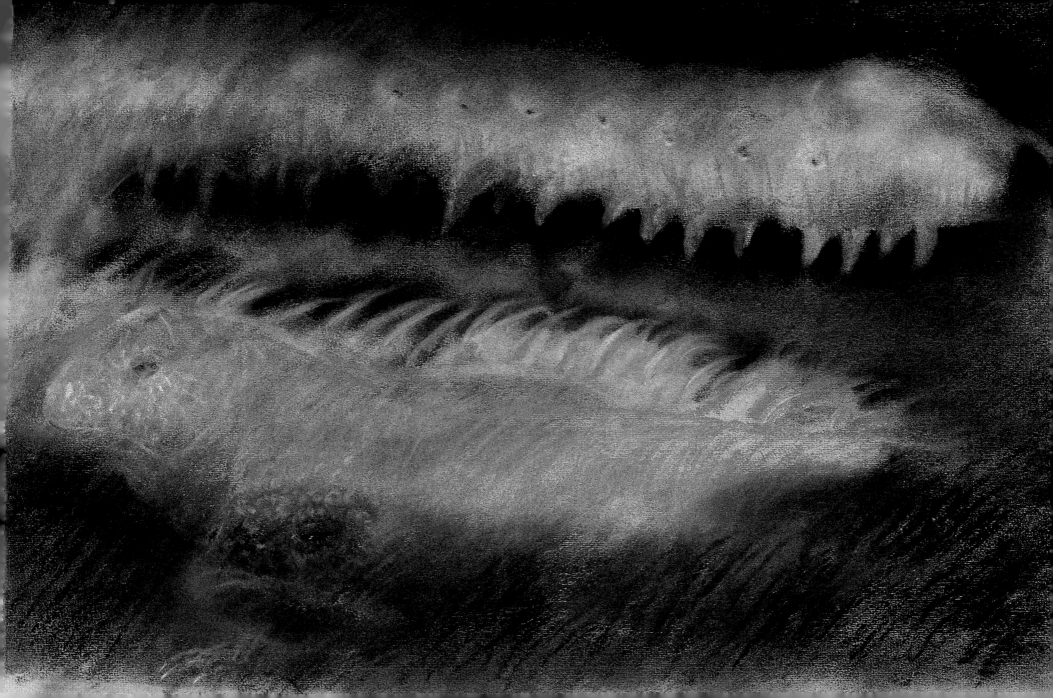

And it was so.

And the evening and the morning were the third day.

And God said, Let there be lights in the firmament of the heaven to divide the day from the night; and let them be for signs, and for seasons, and for days, and years.

And God made two great lights; the greater light to rule the day, and the lesser light to rule the night: he made the stars also.

And God set them in the firmament of the heaven to give light upon the earth: and God saw that it was good.

And the evening and the morning were the fourth day.

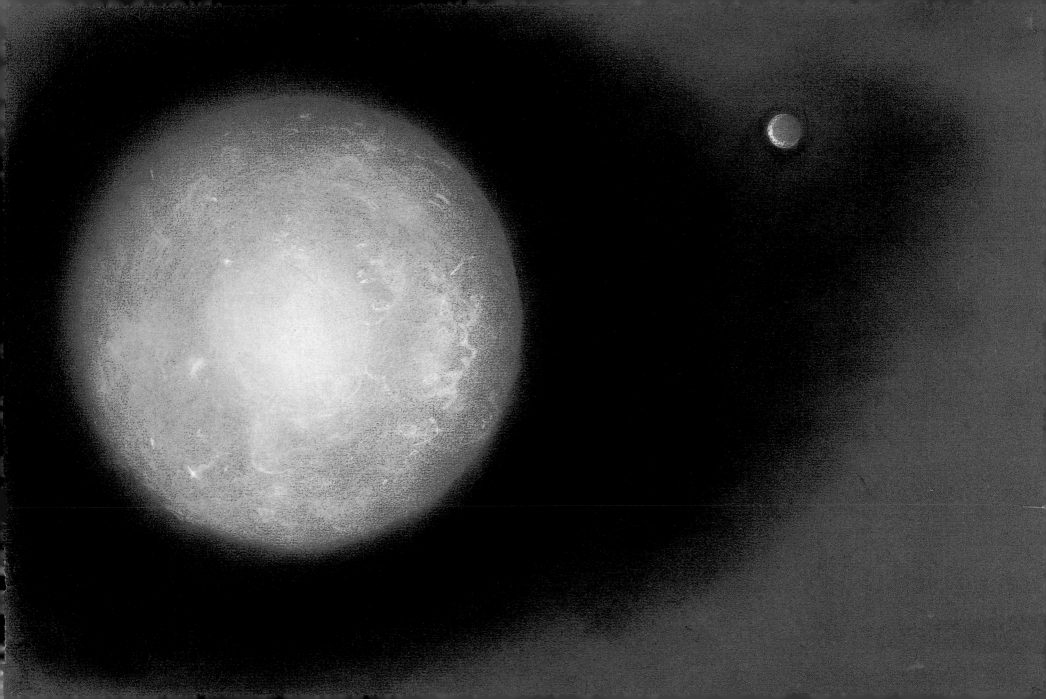

And God said, Let the waters bring forth abundantly the moving creature that hath life, and fowl that may fly above the earth in the open firmament of heaven.

And God created great whales, and every living creature that moveth, and every winged fowl: and God saw that it was good.

And God blessed them, saying, Be fruitful, and multiply, and fill the waters in the seas, and let fowl multiply in the earth.

And the evening and the morning were the fifth day.

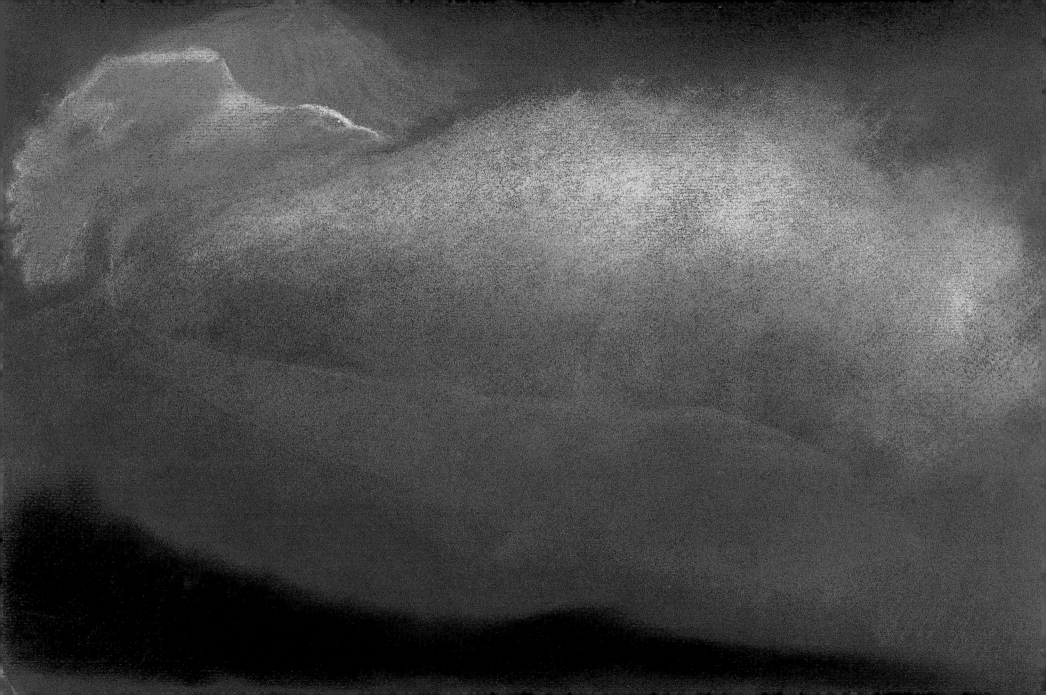

And God said, Let the earth bring forth the living creature, cattle, and creeping thing, and beast of the earth: and it was so.

And God made the beast of the earth, and cattle, and every thing that creepeth upon the earth.

And God said, Let us make man in our image, after our likeness: and let them have dominion over the fish of the sea, and over the fowl of the air, and over the cattle, and over all the earth, and over every creeping thing that creepeth upon the earth.

So God created man in his own image; male and female created he them.

And God blessed them, and God said unto them, Be fruitful, and multiply, and replenish the earth, and subdue it.

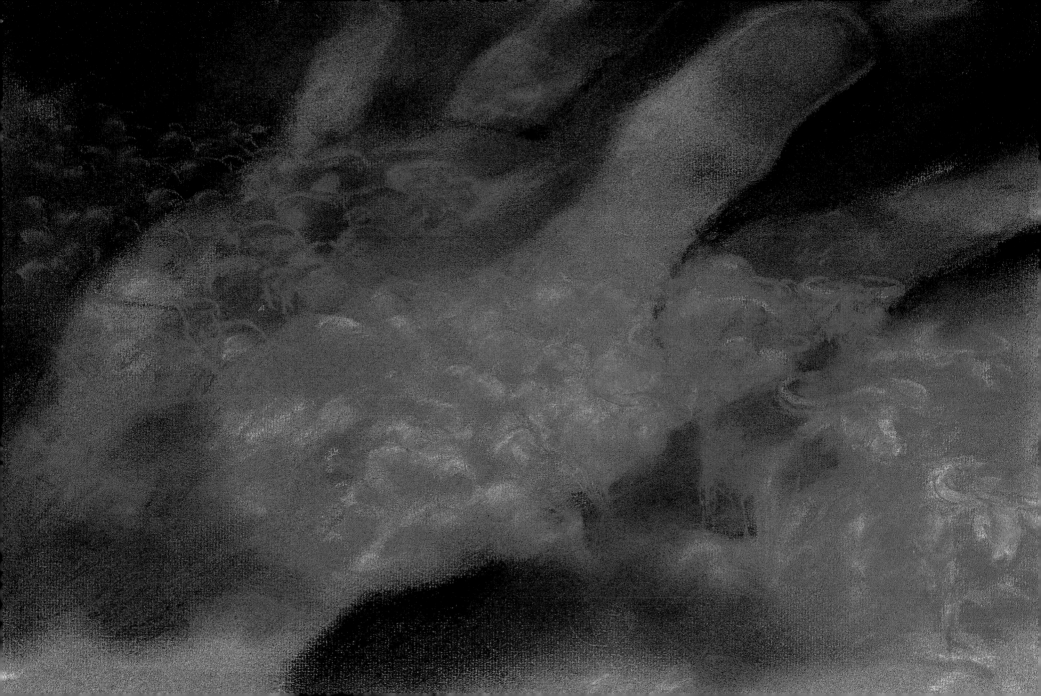

And God saw every thing that he had made, and, behold, it was very good. And the evening and the morning were the sixth day.

Thus the heavens and the earth were finished.

And on the seventh day God ended his work; and he rested.